The Optometrist

By Jenny Giles
Photographs by Lindsay Edwards

I am going to the optometrist.

I can't see very well,
and he is going to look
at my eyes.

Dad is coming with me.

We are in the waiting room.

We look at all the **frames**.

Some of the frames are little.

They are for children like me.

We go into a room with the optometrist.

He talks to me, and I talk to him.

I sit up on the chair.

The optometrist has a **screen** with some letters on it.

The letters at the top are big, and I can read them.
I can't see the little letters very well.

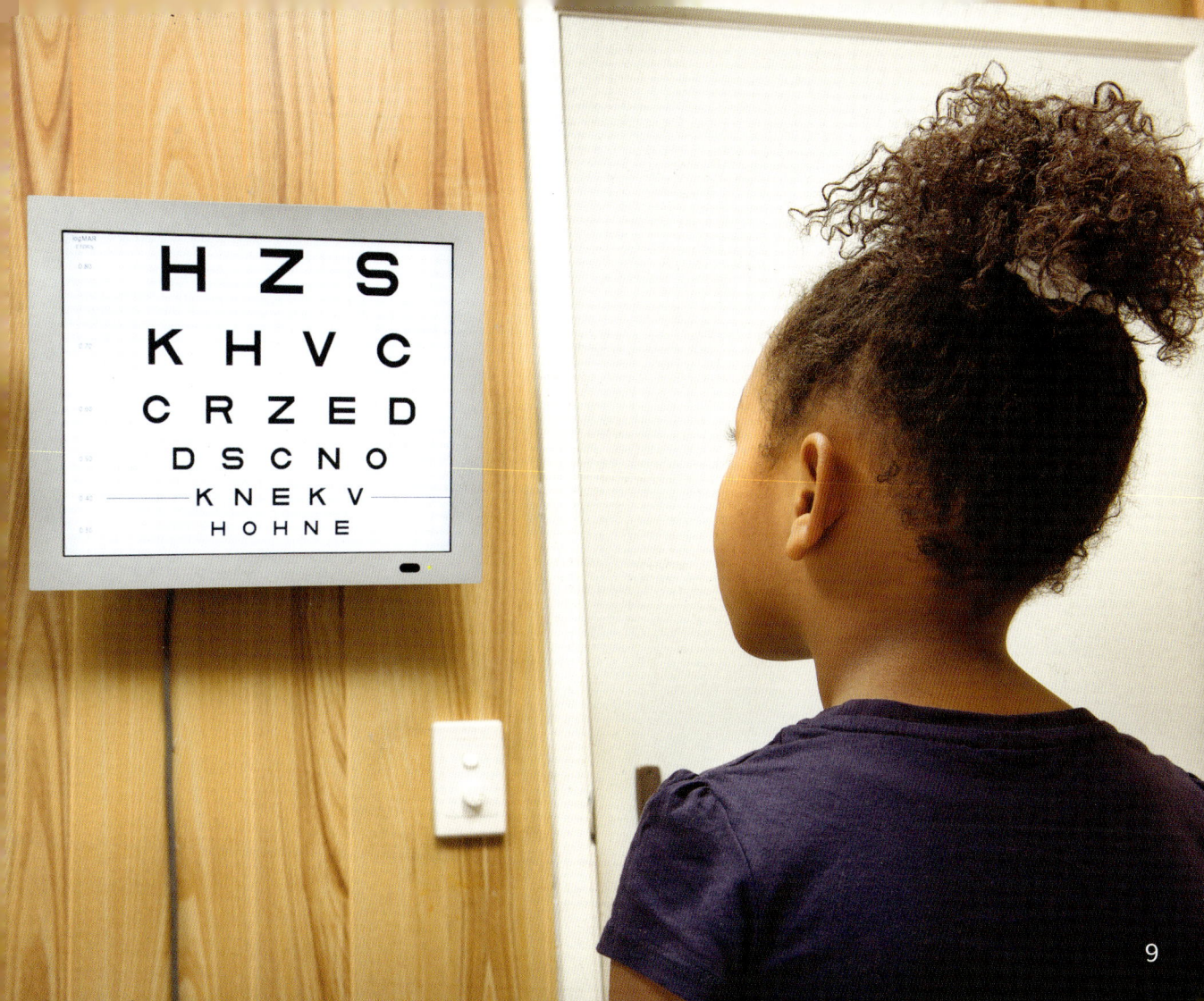

The optometrist has a little **light**.

He looks into my eyes with it.

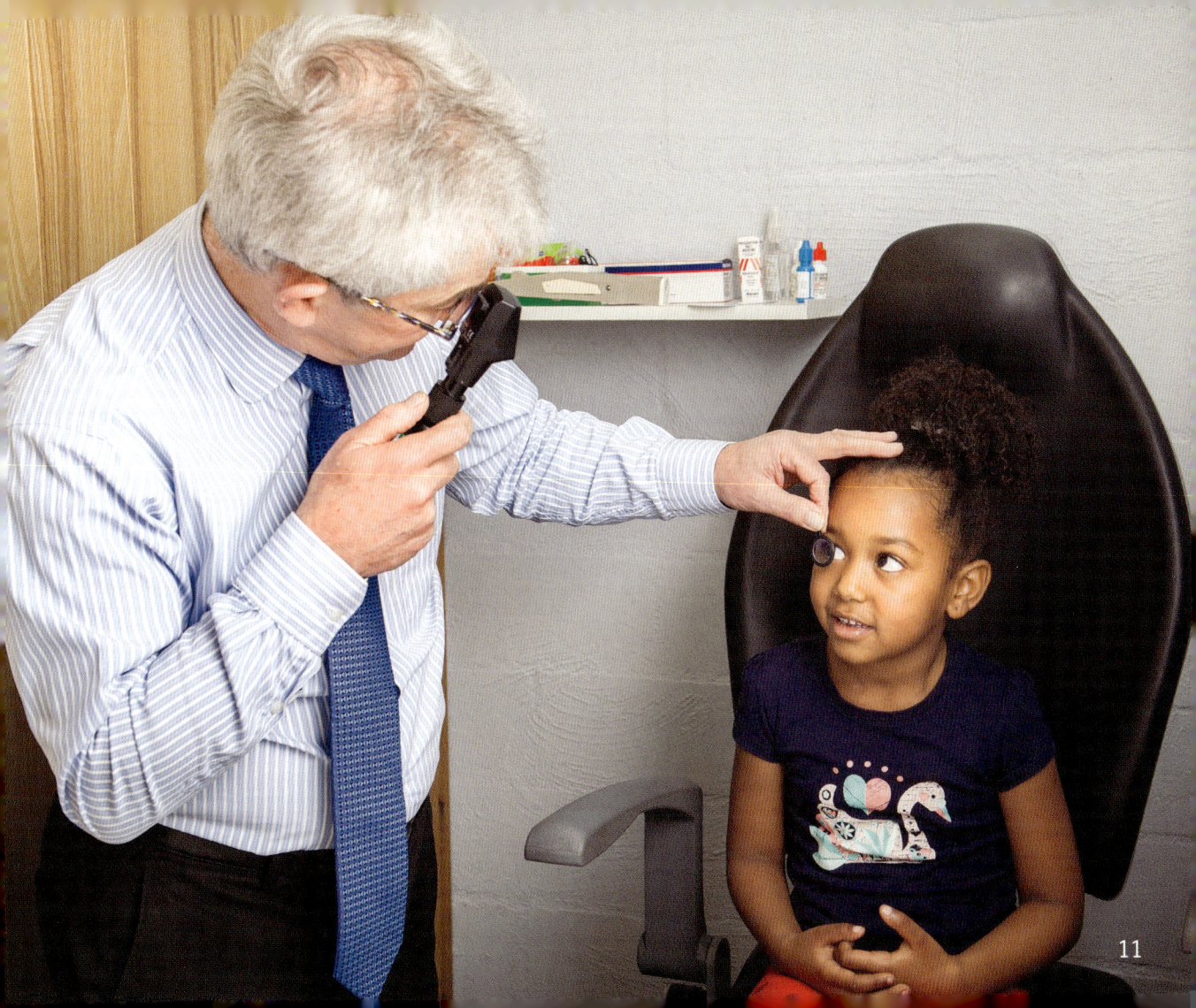

The optometrist puts some **glasses** on me, and I look at the letters again. I can see the little letters now.

I read the letters with one eye. Then, I read them with my other eye.

I am going to get some glasses.

We go back to the waiting room, and I see some little frames that I like.

Dad says they look good on me.
I will get my glasses next week.

Glossary

frames

glasses

light

screen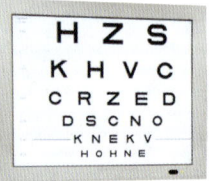